Magical Beasts of The East

Psalm Carnoustie

For all the curious hearts and giggling

adventurers out there

May you always dance like drag-ons,

dream like phoenixes,

and discover magic in the little moments.

This book is your treasure map to kindness,

courage, and laughter.

Now go on, turn the page... your adventure awaits!

Book Cover by Tukotuku Publishing

Illustrations by Tukotuku Publishing

First edition 2025

Print ISBN: 978-1-991339-33-1

Ebook ISBN: 978-1-991339-34-8

Contents

Welcome to Magical Beasts of the East

Taoist Legends for Kids!

Okay, first things first: if you thought this book was just going to be a bunch of old, boring legends told by a dusty old turtle sitting on a rock... think again! Nope, this is not your average storybook. This is a treasure chest full of dancing dragons, giggling phoenixes, cheeky monkeys, and turtles who are way too wise for their own good. Oh, and did we mention the talking bamboo? Yeah, you read that right.

Now, you might be wondering, "What's Taoism, anyway? And what does it have to do with magical creatures?" Great question, my curious friend! Taoism (pronounced Dow-ism, because the "T" decided it was cooler to be silent) is all about balance, kindness, and going with the flow—kind of like a leaf floating down a river or a very chill panda munching on bamboo. And guess what? Every story in this book is packed with these magical Taoist lessons, hidden inside hilarious adventures and heartwarming friendships.

But don't worry—you won't need to sit cross-legged on a mountain or chant mysterious words to understand them. Nope. All you need is an open heart, a sprinkle of imagination, and maybe a snack or two (because even dragons get hungry during storytime).

Inside these pages, you'll meet Sora, the dragon who loves to dance, not roar. There's also Ming, the monkey with the wildest ideas, and Tina, the tortoise who moves slower than ketchup coming out of a bottle—but always gets where she's going. Each chapter is like opening a little window into a world where magic isn't just about spells and potions—it's about kindness, friendship, and finding joy in the little things (like a perfectly ripe banana or a cloud that looks like a bunny).

But here's the best part: these aren't just stories. They're adventures. And you, dear reader, are invited to come along for the ride. So, whether you're reading this under your blanket fort, out loud with your family, or secretly way past bedtime with a flashlight, know this: every story here has a little sprinkle of wisdom, a lot of giggles, and enough magic to keep your imagination soaring.

So, are you ready to dive in? Are you ready to meet dragons who twirl, turtles who tell jokes, and squirrels who organize treasure hunts? Great! Take a deep breath, flip the page, and let's start our adventure into the magical world of Taoist legends.

Ready, set... let's explore!

The Great Dragon of the East

The Dragon Who Loved to Dance

Once upon a time in a vibrant valley, there lived a dragon named Sora, who had a peculiar passion that set her apart from all the other dragons. While most dragons loved to roar, breathe fire, or fly high in the sky, Sora loved to dance! With scales that shimmered like a disco ball, she would twirl and swirl, performing pirouettes that would leave everyone in awe. The other dragons often scratched their heads in confusion. "Why dance when you can fly?" they wondered. But Sora just laughed, "Why fly when you can dance on the clouds?"

One sunny day, Sora decided to throw a grand dance party to showcase her moves. she invited all the creatures of the valley, from the tiniest ants to the tallest trees. But when the day arrived, she noticed that the other dragons were too busy practicing their fire-breathing tricks to come to her party. Feeling a little sad, Sora thought, "Maybe they just don't understand how fun dancing can be!" So, she came up with a brilliant idea. She would mix her dance moves with a bit of fire-breathing to show them how cool it could be!

As the sun set, Sora took a deep breath, puffed out some colorful flames, and started her dance. She spun around, creating a beautiful display of fire that lit up the night sky, making it look like a magical rainbow. The other dragons could not resist the dazzling show! They all flew over, their eyes wide with amazement. "Wow! Look at Sora go!" one dragon exclaimed. Suddenly, they were inspired! The dragons began to join in, trying out their own fire-breathing while dancing. It was a hilarious sight, with some dragons accidentally puffing flames in the wrong direction and others getting tangled up in each other's tails!

The dance party turned into a massive celebration, with everyone laughing and enjoying themselves. Sora felt a warm glow in her heart as she realized that her love for dancing had brought all the creatures together. "You see," Sora said, panting happily, "when we share what we love, we can create joy and friendship!" The dragons nodded, now understanding that dancing wasn't just about moving; it was about connecting and having fun together. They even started to make up a new dance called the "Fire Dragon Shuffle," which involved spinning, hopping, and, of course, lots of fire!

From that day on, the valley was filled with music and laughter, thanks to Sora's love of dance. The dragons learned to embrace each other's passions, whether it was dancing, flying, or even making the best fire-roasted marshmallows. Sora became the valley's official Dance Dragon, and every season, they threw a dance party to celebrate their friendship and creativity. Through her joyful spirit, Sora taught everyone that sometimes, being a little different is what makes life truly magical and fun!

A Friendship with a Little Mouse

Once upon a time in a lush green valley, where the sun shone brighter than a golden coin and the flowers danced like happy fairies, there lived a little mouse named Min. Min was not your ordinary mouse; he had a big heart and an even bigger dream –

to find the tastiest cheese in all of Tao Land. He often imagined himself as a mighty adventurer, like a tiny knight in a cheese-shaped armor. But alas, Min was also quite clumsy, often tripping over his own tiny feet or getting stuck in his own cheese traps!

One sunny day, while Min was on his quest for cheese, he met a wise old turtle named Tao. Tao was taking a leisurely stroll by the river, and he watched Min tumble and roll with great amusement. "Why, hello there, little knight! Are you seeking treasures or just chasing your tail?" he chuckled.

Min, a bit embarrassed but always ready for a laugh, replied, "I'm on a grand adventure to find the biggest cheese in the valley! Care to join me, dear turtle?" And just like that, their friendship began, promising plenty of giggles and unexpected surprises.

As they traveled together, Min learned many valuable Taoist lessons from the slow and steady Tao. "You see, Min," Tao said one day as they watched the clouds float gracefully by, "life is like this river. Sometimes it flows fast, and sometimes it slows down. It's important to be patient and enjoy the journey, especially when cheese is involved!" Min nodded, trying to absorb all the wisdom, even while imagining himself swimming in rivers of cheese. But their adventure wasn't just about cheese; it was also about kindness, as they helped other animals in need along the way.

One day, they came across a family of birds who had lost their way. "Oh no!" chirped the little birds. "We can't find our nest!" Min, feeling brave, squeaked, "Don't worry! We'll help you!" With Tao's guidance, Min climbed the tallest tree, where he spotted the nest nestled between some bright red leaves. Together, they safely guided the little birds home. "You see, Min," said Tao, "true treasure isn't just about cheese; it's about being kind and helping others." Min smiled, realizing that their friendship was the greatest adventure of all.

As the sun began to set, painting the sky in shades of orange and pink, Min and Tao finally spotted a huge wheel of cheese sitting on a pedestal, sparkling like a treasure chest. "This is it! The biggest cheese in Tao Land!" Min squeaked with joy. But as they approached, they noticed a sign that read, "Only those who have shared kindness can enjoy this cheese." Min looked at Tao, and they both laughed, realizing that all their adventures together had led them to this moment. They shared the cheese with their new bird friends and all the animals they had met along the way, proving that true friendship and kindness were the real treasures of their journey.

The Mischievous Monkey

Monkey's Wild Adventures

High up, in a lush and lively forest, there lived a cheeky little monkey named Ming. Ming was not your ordinary monkey; he had a knack for getting into all sorts of mischief. One rainy day, he decided to embark on an adventure that would take him beyond the tallest trees and into the heart of the mystical Tao. As he swung from branch to branch, he chattered excitedly about his plans to explore the world beyond his home, leaving behind a trail of giggles from his friends.

Ming's first stop was the Wise Old Tortoise, who lived by the shimmering pond. The tortoise was known for her slow, thoughtful ways, which made her the perfect friend for a speedy monkey like Ming. "Where are you off to in such a hurry?" asked the tortoise, her voice as slow as molasses. With a gleam in her eye, Ming replied, "I'm going on a wild adventure to find the legendary Bamboo Grove of Giggles!" The tortoise chuckled and said, "Just remember, young monkey, sometimes the best adventures are the ones where you take your time and enjoy the little things." Ming nodded, though he was already imagining all the fun he would have.

As Ming ventured deeper into the forest, he stumbled upon a group of playful squirrels. They were busy having a nut-rolling contest, and Ming couldn't resist joining in. "Look at me, I'm the fastest nut roller in the land!" he boasted. But as he rolled a particularly large acorn, it zoomed past him and knocked over a stack of nuts, sending them flying everywhere! The squirrels squeaked with laughter, and instead of being upset, they invited Ming to help gather the nuts back. Ming learned that sometimes, even when things don't go as planned, friendship and laughter can turn a mishap into a fun adventure.

With his new squirrel friends by his side, Ming continued on his journey. They climbed hills, crossed babbling brooks, and even danced with the fireflies as the sun began to set. Ming realized that the more he laughed and played, the more he understood the Taoist value of kindness. He shared his bananas and acorns with the squirrels, and in return, they shared their favorite stories about the forest. Each tale was filled with lessons about harmony and balance, like how the seasons changed and how even the smallest creatures played a big role in nature.

Finally, after a day filled with laughter, friendship, and silly antics, Ming and his friends arrived at the Bamboo Grove of Giggles. To their surprise, the grove was even more magnificent than they had imagined! The bamboo swayed in the breeze, creating a symphony of rustling leaves that sounded like giggles. Ming realized that the true magic of his adventure was not just in reaching his destination but in all the fun he had along the way. With his heart full of joy and his head spinning with stories, Ming knew that every wild adventure was a chance to learn about the Tao and the importance of kindness, laughter, and friendship in the great big world around him.

The Kindness of the Wise Old Tortoise

In a forest filled with whispering leaves and giggling streams, there lived a wise old tortoise named Tina. Tina was a tortoise like no other; she wore a pair of tiny spectacles perched on her nose, giving her the look of a very serious librarian. But don't be fooled! Tina loved to tell the silliest jokes and would often break into a fit of giggles that echoed through the trees. The other animals loved her for her wisdom, but they adored her for her kindness and her knack for making them laugh.

One day, the animals of the forest gathered for their weekly meeting under the Great Oak Tree. They were worried because a big storm was approaching, and they didn't know how to prepare for it. The birds flapped their wings in a flurry, the rabbits thumped their feet anxiously, and even the wise old owl looked bewildered. Tina, with her glasses sliding down her nose, took a deep breath and said, "Why did the storm bring a suitcase? Because it wanted to pack its thunder!" The animals burst into laughter, and suddenly, the storm didn't seem so scary anymore.

As the winds began to howl, Tina showed everyone how to find shelter. She led them to her cozy cave, where she had plenty of snacks—crunchy leaves and juicy berries. "You can't weather a storm on an empty stomach!" she exclaimed, as she passed around her delicious treats. The animals munched happily while sharing their own silly stories and jokes. Even the grumpy badger, who never smiled, chuckled when Tina told him, "Why don't turtles use computers? Because they're afraid of the mouse!" Laughter filled the cave, and soon, everyone forgot about the storm outside.

After the storm passed, Tina encouraged everyone to come out and see how nature had changed. "Look!" she said, pointing to the rainbow stretching across the sky. "It's nature's way of saying, 'Cheer up, it's time for some fun!'" The animals marveled at the vibrant colors and began to play games, splashing in the puddles and chasing each other around. Tina joined in, moving slowly but surely, proving that you don't have to be fast to have fun. "Why did the tortoise cross the road? To get to the shell-abration on the other side!" she joked, and the animals laughed even harder.

From that day on, Tina was not just known as the wise old tortoise but as the kind-hearted jester of the forest. She taught everyone that kindness and laughter could help them through tough times, just like the storm. The animals learned to appreciate each other and the little things in life, like sharing a snack or telling a joke. And though Tina may have been slow, her heart was always racing with joy, reminding everyone that kindness is the best magic of all.

A Lesson on Sharing Bananas

D eep in a valley filled with colorful flowers and sparkling streams, there lived a cheeky little monkey named Ming. Ming had a special talent: he could swing from tree to tree faster than the blink of an eye! One day, while searching for his favorite snack, he stumbled upon a giant banana tree. "Wowza!" Ming exclaimed, his eyes widening as he spotted the biggest banana he had ever seen, glowing like a treasure under the sun. But there was a tiny problem—this banana was so big that it seemed to have its own gravitational pull, and Ming could hardly lift it!

Ming sat down, scratching his head and thinking, "If I can't eat this banana all by myself, why not share it?" Just then, his friend Tina the Tortoise ambled by, moving at a speed that made a snail look like a racing car. "Hey, Ming! What are you up to?" she asked, her curious eyes peeking out from her shell. "I found this enormous banana! Do you want to help me eat it?" Ming replied, his voice bursting with excitement. Tina's eyes lit up like fireflies. "Of course, but how can we get it down from the tree?" she wondered, looking at the towering fruit as if it were a mountain.

Ming thought hard and then had a brilliant idea. "Let's call our friends! With all of us working together, we can shake the tree and make the banana fall!" Tina nodded, and they quickly gathered their friends: Brucie the Bunny, who could hop higher than any other bunny, and Fred the Fox, who was known for his clever tricks. Together, they formed a plan. Brucie started to bounce against the tree while Fred ran in circles, making funny faces to cheer everyone on. Tina clapped her little feet in rhythm, singing a silly song about bananas. The tree shook and wobbled, and with one last mighty bounce from Brucie, the giant banana fell right into their arms!

As they gathered around the banana, Ming said, "Now that we have it, let's cut it into pieces so everyone can have a share!" But just as they were about to dig in, a wise old owl named Oliver swooped down. "Hold on, young ones! Remember, sharing isn't just about splitting food; it's about friendship and kindness too!" The friends looked at each other, realizing that sharing the banana was not just about the fruit, but also about the fun they had together. They laughed, danced, and told stories while munching on the delicious banana slices, feeling their hearts grow warmer with each bite.

So, from then on, Ming and his friends learned a valuable lesson about sharing. They discovered that sharing brought them closer together, created joy, and even more fun adventures. Whenever they found something special, they made sure to include everyone. So, if you ever find a giant banana or any treasure, remember the tale of Ming the monkey and his friends, and think about how wonderful it is to share with others! After all, life is sweeter when enjoyed together, and who knows what magical adventures await when you share a little kindness?

The Wise Old Owl

The Owl Who Knew Too Much

In a cozy little forest where the trees whispered secrets, there lived an owl named Oliver. Oliver was not your everyday owl; he had a knack for knowing everything about the world around him. He could tell you which way the wind was blowing, what the squirrels were up to, and even the best hiding spots for acorns. His friends often joked that he was the "wisest of the wise," but sometimes they thought he knew just a bit too much!

One bright morning, while perched on his favorite branch, Oliver overheard a couple of rabbits discussing a mysterious treasure hidden deep in the woods. His big, round eyes sparkled with excitement. "Treasure? Oh, I must investigate!" he hooted, flapping his wings dramatically. The rabbits giggled and said, "You may know a lot, Oliver, but you'd better watch out for trouble!" But Oliver, full of confidence and a dash of mischief, ignored their warning and set off on his grand adventure.

As Oliver swooped through the trees, he met Benny the Bear, who was busy picking berries for his breakfast. "Hey, Benny! Have you heard about the treasure?" he asked, his feathers ruffling in anticipation. Benny chuckled, "Oh, Oliver! You should know that sometimes treasure comes with a side of trouble!" But Oliver just laughed and continued on his quest, imagining all the shiny goodies he would find. Little did he know, his adventure was about to take a twist!

Deeper into the woods, Oliver stumbled upon a rickety old bridge that looked like it had seen better days. He thought, "I know how to cross this! Just hop and flap!" But as he hopped, the bridge creaked and groaned, making sounds that could scare a buffalo! Suddenly, one of the planks snapped, and down went Oliver into a pile of leaves with a squawk! All the forest creatures rushed to see what had happened. Oliver, with leaves sticking out of his feathers, realized that maybe knowing too much wasn't always a good thing!

His friends helped him up, and together they shared a hearty laugh over Oliver's mishap. "You see, Oliver," said Benny, "sometimes it's better to listen to your friends than to rush into things, even if you think you know it all!" Oliver nodded, feeling a warm glow in his heart. He may have known a lot, but he learned that friendship and kindness were the true treasures of the forest. With a newfound sense of balance, Oliver decided that sometimes, some mysteries are best shared with friends, and maybe, just maybe, he didn't need to know everything after all!

The Search for Friendship

In the forest known as the Whispering Woods, there lived a little dragon named Sora. she had sparkly scales that shimmered like a disco ball! But Sora didn't do "ordinary." and was one of the shiniest creatures in the forest, Sora felt a little lonely. You see, all the other animals thought she was too flashy and often called her "Sora the Show-off." Sora sighed, wishing she could find a friend who appreciated her sparkle rather than shunned it.

On a not so sunny day, while practicing her fabulous twirls and sparkly spins, Sora spotted a group of animals gathered around a bubbling brook. Curious as a cat, she floated over, hoping to join in on the fun. "What are you all doing?" she asked, her scales glinting in the sunlight. The animals looked at her with wide eyes and whispered, "We're playing hide-and-seek, but we can't hide with you around. You're just too shiny!" Sora's heart sank like a rock.she wanted to play, but her sparkle seemed to be the very thing keeping her from making friends.

Feeling a bit down, Sora decided to take a stroll and clear her mind. As she wandered through the forest, she stumbled upon an old tortoise named Tina. Tina was trying to reach a particularly juicy leaf that was just out of her reach, Sora who was always eager to help, swooped down and offered, "I can help you with that!" Tina looked up, squinting at the dazzling light show happening above her. "Oh, fine! Just don't blind me with your sparkles!" she grumbled. With one swift flick of her tail, Sora nudged the branch, sending the tasty leaf tumbling down. Tina munched happily, and Sora's heart did a little dance.

Sora and Tina became the most unlikely of friends. They spent their days exploring the forest, with Sora sparkling like a star, guiding Tina through the thick brush. Tina often joked, "I'm the brains, and you're the brawn!" Sora laughed, realizing that her sparkle was not a burden but a blessing. Together, they taught the other animals that friendship didn't depend on being the same; it was about helping each other and finding joy in differences. Soon, the other animals began to join in their adventures, and Sora's sparkle became a shining beacon of fun rather than a reason to hide.

In time, Sora learned that true friendship was not about blending in but about celebrating what makes each of us unique. She discovered that kindness and sharing could draw everyone together, no matter how sparkly or dull they were. The forest echoed with laughter, and Sora's heart felt as bright as her scales. The animals learned that, like the balance of yin and yang, friendship flourished when they embraced each other's differences. And so, in the magical Whispering Woods, Sora the dragon and Tina the tortoise became legends of friendship, reminding everyone that sometimes, it takes a little sparkle and a lot of kindness to create the best adventures.

The Nighttime Tale of Kindness

In a quiet forest under a moonlit sky, where the trees whispered secrets and the stars twinkled like playful fireflies, there lived a curious little fox named Fred. Fred had a knack for getting into trouble, mostly because he couldn't help but poke his nose into everything. One night, while wandering around looking for snacks (he had a serious weakness for berries), he stumbled upon a peculiar sight: a grumpy old hare named Trev, who had somehow gotten his ear stuck in a bush. Fred couldn't help but giggle a little at the sight. "Trev, you look like a pancake stuck in a pancake maker!" he chuckled.

But Fred's laughter quickly turned to concern when he realized Trev was in a pickle—well, a bush, actually. "Oh no, I should help him!" he thought. With all his might, Fred tried to pull Trev free, but all he managed to do was get himself tangled in the same bush. "Now we're both pancakes!" Trev grumbled, his voice muffled by leaves. Fred laughed again, but this time it was more of a nervous giggle. "How are we going to get out of this one?" he asked. Just then, a wise old owl named Oliver swooped down from a branch above, his feathers ruffled with amusement.

"Why don't you both try a little kindness?" Oliver suggested, tilting his head as if he knew a secret. "You see, the best way to solve a problem is to work together."

Fred scratched his head, wondering how that would help. "But I'm stuck!" he exclaimed. Oliver gave a knowing wink. "Sometimes, being stuck is just a chance to make a new friend." With that, Fred and Trev began to chat and share stories about their adventures. The more they talked, the more they realized they actually had a lot in common—like their love for berries and their dislike for rainy days!

As they laughed and shared tales of their escapades, something magical happened. The bush that had once held them captive began to loosen its grip! With a final tug and a lot of giggles, Fred and Trev wriggled free, tumbling onto the soft grass below. "We did it!" Fred squealed, doing a little dance. "Thanks to kindness, we're free! And you know what? I think we make a pretty good team!" Trev nodded, his grumpy demeanor replaced with a bright, toothy smile. "Who knew being stuck could lead to such a wonderful friendship? Maybe next time, I'll stick to eating leaves instead of getting stuck in bushes!"

From that night on, Fred and Trev became the best of friends, exploring the forest together and helping other animals in need. They learned that kindness could turn any frown upside down, and laughter was the best glue to stick friendships together. And so, under the gentle glow of the moon and the twinkling stars, their nighttime tale of kindness spread throughout the forest, reminding all the creatures that helping one another was the most magical adventure of all!

The Dance-off in the Clouds

High above the bustling world, where the clouds are as fluffy as cotton candy, a group of magical creatures gathered for the most exciting event of the year—the Dance-off in the Clouds! Everyone from the sassy sky turtles to the flamboyant feathered phoenixes was ready to show off their best moves. The air was filled with giggles and the sweet scent of cloudberries, a favorite snack for all. It was a day when even the grumpiest old dragon couldn't resist a little shimmy and shake!

As the sun peeked through the fluffy white clouds, the grand-master of ceremonies, a wise old owl named Oliver, fluffed up his feathers and hooted with excitement. "Welcome, friends! Today we will celebrate friendship and kindness through dance!" he declared, his voice echoing across the sky. The creatures cheered, and a herd of fluffy cloud bunnies started to hop in rhythm, their ears flopping like floppy pancakes. Even the clouds seemed to sway as if they were joining in on the fun!

First up was Brian the Sky Turtle. Brian was known for being slow, but today he had a plan! He wobbled to the front and began to spin like a top, his shell gleaming in the sunlight. The other creatures couldn't help but laugh as he twirled and twirled, turning in circles until he became a whirlwind of fluff and giggles. "Look at me! I'm a tornado!" he joked, and the crowd roared with

laughter. Brian reminded everyone that sometimes, being slow
and steady could lead to the best
dance moves—especially when
you add a sprinkle of humor!

Next, it was Frank the Phoenix's
turn. With his fiery feathers and
dazzling dance skills, he soared
into the sky with a whoosh! Frank
performed flips and twirls, leaving trails of sparkling fire behind
him. The other creatures watched
in awe, but then, oh no! Frank
accidentally flew too high and
got tangled in a bunch of fluffy
clouds. "Help! I'm cloud-stuck!" he
squawked, and everyone burst

into laughter. But Brian, being the kind-hearted turtle, slowly waddled over to help him out, proving that friendship is all about lending a hand—especially when your friends are stuck in the clouds!

Finally, it was time for a group dance-off! Oliver the Owl called out, "Let's show the world how we can work together!" The creatures formed circles, and soon they were hopping, spinning, and flapping in perfect harmony. They danced as one big happy cloud family, celebrating their differences and the joy of being together. Laughter filled the sky and sparkled like stars as they twirled and twisted, reminding everyone that kindness and friendship could make even the silliest dance-off an unforgettable adventure. And so, in the sky where the clouds danced, the magical beasts learned that the true magic of Taoism lay not just in the dance, but in the love and laughter shared along the way.

The Journey of the Magical Carp

The Carp's Dream of Becoming a Dragon

Deep in a shimmering river filled with glimmering fish and singing frogs, there lived a carp named Carl. Carl was a one of a kind carp and he had big dreams. Every night, while his fishy friends were busy munching on algae and playing hide-and-seek among the rocks, Carl stared at the stars and dreamed of becoming a dragon. "Oh, how magnificent it would be!" he thought. "To soar through the clouds and breathe fire!" Of course, he didn't have a clue about what fire was, but it sounded super cool!

On a particularly wet day, while Carl was practicing his dragon roars— which sounded more like a squeaky toy than anything fierce—he met a wise old duck named Terry. Terry chuckled at Carl's enthusiasm and said, "Young carp, do you know the story of the Dragon Gate?" Carl shook his head, his fins flapping excitedly. Terry explained that all carp, just like him, could leap out of the water and swim upstream to a magical gate. If a carp could jump high enough, it would transform into a magnificent dragon! Carl could hardly contain his giggles. "I'm going to be the first carp-dragon ever!" he declared, splashing water everywhere.

With newfound determination, Carl decided it was time to train.

He enlisted the help of his friends: a clever frog named Nigel and a speedy little fish named Finn. Together, they devised a training plan that involved jumping over lily pads, racing against the current, and even practicing dramatic poses on the riverbanks. Carl took every practice session seriously, until one day, he flopped right out of the water and landed—splash!—on a sunny rock, startling a passing bird who squawked, "What in the world?" Carl just laughed, "I'm training to be a dragon!" The bird rolled its eyes and flew away, probably thinking Carl was a bit nuts.

As the days went by, Carl grew stronger and more confident. Finally, the day arrived for the big jump to the Dragon Gate. Carl's heart raced as he swam upstream, his friends cheering him on. "You can do it, Carl! You're the best carp-dragon we know!" With one last push, Carl leaped out of the water, soaring high into the air. He felt like he was flying! But just then, he realized that he was still just a carp in mid-air. He landed with a splash back into the river, surrounded by bubbles and laughter from Nigel and Finn.

Carl surfaced, a bit dazed but full of giggles. "I guess I'm not a dragon yet!" he laughed. But just then, he noticed something magical. As he looked around, he saw how his friends were still there, cheering him on, and how much fun they had together. In that moment, Carl understood something important: it wasn't about becoming a dragon; it was about the adventure, the friendship, and enjoying the journey. From that day on, Carl may not have turned into a dragon, but he sure became the happiest carp in the river, proving that sometimes, dreams can change, and that's perfectly okay!

The Friends Met Along the Way

As the sun peeked over the mountains, a little boy named Li set off on an adventure through the enchanted forest, where magical beasts roamed freely. With a twinkle in his eye and a spring in his step, Li was ready to meet some new friends.

But little did he know, the forest was full of quirky creatures who loved to play tricks and share tales! Just as Li stepped onto the path, he stumbled over a fluffy, orange creature that looked like a giant ball of yarn. "Watch where you're going!" it squeaked, fluffing up its fur. "I'm Fred, the playful fox! Let's race to the river and see who's faster!"

Li laughed and accepted the challenge. Off they went, dashing through the trees, dodging branches like nimble ninjas. Fred zigzagged, darting left and right, while Li kept his eyes on the prize.

But just as they reached the riverbank, they both tripped and landed in a huge pile of leaves! "Well, that wasn't part of the plan!" Li chuckled, shaking leaves from his hair. Fred just rolled around in the leaves, giggling. "This is the best kind of mess! You know, the forest is always about having fun and being kind, just like Taoism teaches us!"

As they brushed off the leaves in the warm sun, they noticed a shimmering light coming from behind a nearby tree. Curious, they tiptoed closer and discovered a tiny dragon with shimmering scales that glimmered like rainbows. "Hello, I'm Sora!" the dragon said, puffing out a small cloud of sparkles. Sora was looking for someone to help him find his lost treasure – a magical pearl that could make anyone's wishes come true! Li and Fred jumped at the chance to help their new friend. "A treasure hunt? Count us in!" shouted Li, his eyes sparkling with excitement.

The trio set off, following the trail of twinkling dust left by the magical pearl. Along the way, they encountered a wise old tortoise named Tina who loved to tell stories. "Do you know why friends are like the moon and stars?" she asked, her eyes twinkling with mischief. "Because they brighten your darkest days!" Li giggled at the silly tortoise and realized that every friend they made was helping them grow, just like the seasons change and bring new adventures. The more friends they had, the more fun they had together, and that was a treasure worth more than a pearl!

Finally, after a day filled with laughter, stories, and teamwork, they found the magical pearl nestled in a bed of flowers. Sora was overjoyed and promised to use its magic for good. "Let's make a wish together!" she exclaimed. They all closed their eyes and wished for more adventures and friendships. When they opened their eyes, they were surrounded by sparkling lights, each one representing a new friend waiting to be met. Li realized that the real magic wasn't just in the pearl but in the friends they had met along the way. And just like that, their journey continued, filled with kindness, laughter, and a whole lot of fun!

The Splashes of Success

In a beautiful forest filled with giggles and sneezes, lived a cheerful little frog named Nigel. This frog? Totally one of a kind.; he dreamed of becoming the greatest jumper in the entire forest. Every day, he practiced hopping over leaves, logs, and even the occasional sleepy snail. His friends, a wise old tortoise named Tina and a quirky squirrel named Sid, cheered him on, but they also couldn't help but giggle at his wobbly jumps that often ended in splashes!

One sunny day, Nigel decided it was time to show off his incredible jumping skills. He announced to everyone, "Today, I shall jump over the Great Log of Destiny!" His friends gasped in awe, while the log, who was actually quite grumpy, moaned, "Oh no, not another one of Nigel's crazy ideas!" But Nigel was determined. He took a deep breath, wiggled his little froggy toes, and prepared for the biggest leap of his life. With a mighty bounce, he soared through the air like a superhero frog, until—oops! He landed smack in the middle of a puddle, splashing water everywhere and drenching all the nearby critters.

Instead of feeling embarrassed, Nigel burst into laughter. "Well, that wasn't quite the plan!" he chuckled, shaking the water off his shiny skin. Tina, who had been watching with wide eyes, couldn't help but laugh too. "You certainly made a splash, Nigel! Maybe you're not the greatest jumper, but you sure know how to have fun!" Sid added, "And you've given us all a reason to smile today!" Nigel realized that sometimes, it's not about being the best at something, but about having a good time with friends and making memories.

As the sun began to set, the trio gathered by the shimmering pond, where the water sparkled like tiny stars. They shared stories about their day, and Nigel learned something important: success isn't just about landing the perfect jump; it's about the joy of trying and the laughter shared along the way. Tina reminded him, "In Taoism, we believe in the journey, not just the destination. Every splash is a step toward understanding ourselves and our friends!" Nigel nodded, feeling warm and fuzzy inside as he appreciated his friends even more.

That night, as the moonlight danced on the water, Nigel realized that every splash he made was a success in its own way. He had brought happiness to his friends and had fun along the journey. From that day on, whenever he attempted a jump and landed in a puddle, he would just laugh and say, "Another splash of success!" And so, Nigel continued to leap, splash, and spread joy throughout the forest, reminding everyone that the best adventures are filled with laughter, friendship, and a little bit of silliness.

The Enchanted Peach Tree

The Peaches of Friendship

O nce upon a time in the enchanting land of the East, there lived a wise old turtle named Tao. Tao was not just any turtle; he had a special talent for growing the juiciest peaches in the entire forest. These peaches were magical! They sparkled in the sunlight and tasted like sunshine mixed with sweetness. Every summer, animals from far and wide would come to Tao's peach tree, hoping for a taste of his famous fruit and, of course, the joy of friendship.

One day, a cheeky little monkey named Ming swung down from his tree, his eyes twinkling with mischief. "Hey, Tao! I heard your peaches are the best in the world! Can I have one?" Tao smiled and nodded, but with a twinkle in his eye, he said, "Of course, but first you have to help me pick them!" Ming scratched his head. Picking peaches sounded a lot less fun than eating them! However, he agreed because he knew that sharing an adventure with Tao would be a peach of a time.

As they picked peaches, Ming suddenly had a brilliant idea. "Let's have a peach party! We can invite all our friends!" Tao laughed, "That's a great idea! But remember, a true friend shares not just the peaches but also the fun of making them." So, they gathered their pals—Brucie the bunny, Benny the bear, and Lila the small owl. Each friend brought their own special talent: Brucie brought his hopping skills, Benny his strength, and Lila her stories about magical places. They giggled and worked together, making the peach party the best event ever!

When the day of the party arrived, the forest was filled with laughter and the sweet smell of peaches. The friends set up games, shared stories, and, of course, munched on the delicious peaches. Ming, who had initially only wanted to eat, realized that sharing with friends made the peaches taste even better! As they played, they discovered that kindness and team-work were the true magic behind Tao's famous peaches. The animals learned that friendship grows sweeter when shared, just like the peaches from Tao's tree.

As the sun began to set, painting the sky with colors as beautiful as the peaches, Tao looked at his friends and smiled. "Remember, my dear friends, it's not just about the peaches. It's about the laughter, the adventures, and the kindness we share. That's the true magic of friendship!" And with that, the animals agreed, their hearts full of joy. They promised to always share their own special gifts, just like Tao shared his magical peaches. From that day on, the forest was not only known for its delicious peaches but also for the laughter and friendship that blossomed among its magical creatures.

The Adventure of the Hungry Bear

O nce upon a time in a magical forest, there lived a bear named Benny who was as hungry as a bear could possibly be! Benny was a bear with a twist; he had a fluffy coat that shimmered in the sunlight and a big, goofy grin that made all the forest animals laugh. One morning, Benny woke up with a rumble in his tummy that sounded like a thunderstorm. "Oh dear," he grumbled, scratching his belly, "I need food, and I need it now!" With a determined twinkle in his eye, Benny set off on an adventure to find the tastiest treats in the whole forest.

As Benny waddled along, he came across his friend, Tina the Tortoise, who was munching on a delicious patch of clover. "Hey, Tina! Have you seen any snacks that could fill my big bear belly?" Benny asked, his voice rumbling like a bass drum. Tina chuckled,

"Well, there's a berry bush just beyond the creek! But watch out for the mischievous squirrel, Sid—he loves to play tricks!" Benny, being the brave bear he was, laughed and said, "A little squirrel can't stop a hungry bear! Let's go, Tina!" And off they went, Benny bounding and Tina slowly plodding behind.

When they reached the berry bush, Benny's eyes sparkled with excitement. Bright, juicy berries hung from the branches, just waiting to be gobbled up! But before Benny could take a bite, Sid the Squirrel zipped down from a tree, wearing a tiny crown made of acorns. "Not so fast, Benny!" he squeaked, doing a little dance. "To eat these berries, you must answer my riddle!" Benny scratched his head, thinking, "A riddle? This could be fun!" Sid grinned mischievously, "What has keys but can't open locks?" Benny pondered, and after a moment, he yelled, "A piano!" Sid laughed so hard he nearly fell off his branch. "Alright, you win! Feast away, my fluffy friend!"

Benny devoured the berries with gusto, his tummy finally feeling happy. Tina joined in, munching on clover while Sid scampered around, tossing berries in the air like confetti. The three friends laughed and played, sharing stories and jokes. Benny realized that while his belly was now full, the best part of the adventure was the fun and friendship he shared with Tina and Sid. "You know," Benny said with a belly full of berries, "it's not just about filling your tummy. It's about filling your heart with laughter and kindness, too!"

After their berry feast, Benny, Tina, and Sid decided to make a game of it. They created a berry treasure hunt, hiding berries around the forest for each other to find. As they played, they learned about working together and helping each other, just like true friends do. Benny realized that adventure is even better when shared with friends, and kindness is the real treasure of any journey. With the sun setting in the sky, the three friends headed home, their hearts light and their bellies happy, ready for more adventures to come!

Sharing the First Bite

Deep In a forest where the trees danced with the wind, there lived a cheeky little monkey named Ming. Ming loved to play pranks on his friends, especially when it came to food. One afternoon, he spotted a juicy, ripe mango hanging from a branch. It was the biggest mango he had ever seen! His eyes sparkled with mischief as he carefully planned how to share it with his friends. But not just any sharing—he wanted to make it the most spectacular sharing event ever!

Ming gathered his friends: a wise old turtle named , a graceful deer named Dandelion, and a chatty parrot named . "Let's have a feast!" he announced, waving the mango in the air like a trophy. "But first, we need to make it special!" His friends were puzzled. "What's so special about a mango?" asked Tofu, who was already thinking about his favorite seaweed snacks. Ming grinned and replied, "We'll have a sharing ceremony! I'll take the first bite, and then everyone else can have a piece!" The friends giggled, imagining the grand event.

On the day of the feast, Ming decorated the area with leaves and flowers, creating a beautiful spot under a big tree. He wore a crown made of twigs and announced, "Welcome to the Great Mango Feast!" Dandelion clapped her hooves, while Pippa squawked in delight. But as Ming prepared to take the first bite, he noticed Tofu slowly munching on his favorite seaweed snack in the corner. "Hey, Tofu! Are you not excited about the mango?" Ming teased. Tofu smiled and said, "Oh, I'm just trying to enjoy my snack first. Mangos are good, but seaweed is the best!" Ming realized he needed to make this sharing even more fun.

With a wink, Ming had a brilliant idea. "Alright, how about we play a game? Whoever can tell the funniest joke gets to take the next bite after me!" The friends erupted in laughter, eager to compete. Tofu shared a joke about a turtle who couldn't find his shell, Dandelion told a silly story about a deer that wore glasses, and Pippa paraded around, mimicking other animals. When it was Ming's turn, he jumped up and said, "What do you call a monkey who loves bananas? A 'peel'-o-fun!" The friends roared with laughter, and even Tofu chuckled, shaking his head at the silliness.

Finally, it was time for Ming to take the first bite. With a dramatic flourish, he took a huge chomp, mango mush flying everywhere! "Mmm, this is the best mango ever!" he declared, wiping mango bits off his face. His friends couldn't help but giggle at the sight. Then, with wide smiles, they each got a piece of the mango. As they munched together, they realized that sharing wasn't just about the food—it was about the laughter, the fun, and the joy of being together. In that moment, they learned that friendship, kindness, and a little humor made every bite taste even better.

The Laughing Phoenix

The Phoenix Who Couldn't Stop Giggles

In a bright and colorful forest where the trees danced with the wind, there lived a peculiar phoenix named Frank. Frank was not your ordinary phoenix; while most phoenixes were known for their majestic beauty and fiery feathers, Frank had a giggle that could set the whole forest aflame—without any fire! Whenever he tried to soar through the sky with his friends, he would burst into fits of laughter, and his giggles would echo through the valleys, causing even the grumpiest of creatures to chuckle. The other animals loved Frank for his laughter, but they often wondered if he would ever stop giggling long enough to show off his dazzling wings.

One sunny morning, all the animals gathered for the Great Forest Race. The wise old tortoise

Tina, who was the referee, announced, "Today, we will see who can fly the highest!" Frank was excited and wanted to join, but every time he imagined zooming up into the sky, he couldn't help but giggle uncontrollably. "I'm going to win this race!" he declared, but the moment he flapped his wings, a fit of giggles erupted, sending him wobbling and tumbling instead. The rabbits rolled on the ground with laughter, while the birds chirped in delight, "Look at Frank go! He's flying funny!"

Determined to focus, Frank decided to practice in secret. He perched on a branch, took a deep breath, and closed his eyes. "No giggling, no giggling," he whispered to himself, but as soon as he opened his eyes, he spotted Sid the squirrel doing a silly dance below. Frank burst into giggles again, and the branch shook with his laughter. "Why can't I just be serious for once?" he sighed. But deep down, he realized that his giggles made others happy. The animals loved his antics, and maybe, just maybe, laughter was a special kind of magic too.

Finally, the day of the race arrived. As Frank stood at the starting line, his heart raced faster than a cheetah. With a deep breath, he reminded himself of all the fun he brought to his friends. "I should just be me!" he thought. When the race began, Frank took off, and just as he expected, the giggles bubbled up again. But this time, instead of wobbling, Frank soared higher and higher, his laughter ringing through the air like the most beautiful song. The other animals cheered, and instead of feeling embarrassed, Frank embraced his joyful giggles, realizing they were his superpower.

As the race came to an end, Frank didn't win, but he was the star of the show. The other animals celebrated him with cheers, and the wise old tortoise declared, "Today, we learned that laughter is just as important as winning!" Frank beamed with pride. He understood that true friends appreciate you for who you are, even if you can't stop giggling. From that day forward, Frank embraced his giggles, knowing they spread kindness and joy throughout the forest. And so, the phoenix who couldn't stop giggles became the heart of the forest, reminding everyone that sometimes, laughter is the best adventure of all.

A Journey to the Rainbow

In a land not too far away, where the mountains tickled the sky and rivers danced with joy, there lived a curious little rabbit named Brucie. One sunny day, Brucie overheard a wise old tortoise named Tina talking about a magical rainbow that appeared only once in a blue moon. "What's so special about this rainbow?" Brucie wondered, twitching his fluffy ears. Tina chuckled and said, "Oh, dear Brucie! This rainbow is said to grant one wish, and it can only be found by those who believe in the magic of friendship and kindness." Brucie's eyes sparkled brighter than the sun as he decided right then and there: he was going to find that rainbow!

Brucie hopped along the winding path, chanting "Rainbow, rainbow, here I come!" He met a colorful parrot named Pippa, who was busy practicing her dance moves. "Hey, Brucie! What's the rush?" Pippa squawked, flapping her wings dramatically. "I'm on a quest to find the magical rainbow!" Brucie exclaimed. Pippa's feathers ruffled with excitement. "Count me in! I could use a little adventure and a chance to show off my dance moves!" With a flurry of feathers and fur, the two new friends set off, laughing and sharing stories, as the sun peeked through the trees like a shy little child.

As they journeyed deeper into the forest, they stumbled upon a grumpy old badger named Brad, who was trying unsuccessfully to open a jar of honey.

"What's wrong, Mr. Badger?" Brucie asked, twitching his nose. "I can't get this jar open! It's so sticky!" grumbled. Brucie and Pippa looked at each other and giggled. "Let us help you!" Together, they pulled, tugged, and finally popped the jar open, sending honey flying everywhere! Brad was covered in sticky goo, but soon he was laughing too. "Thank you, little friends! You've made my day sweeter!" With a belly full of honey and hearts full of joy, the trio continued on their quest, their friendship growing stronger with every sticky step.

After a while, they reached a sparkling stream that shimmered like a thousand diamonds. The rainbow was rumored to be hidden just beyond it. However, the stream had no bridge! Brucie scratched his head, feeling a little unsure. "How will we cross?" he asked. Pippa soared above, spotting a few large leaves floating by. "Let's make a leaf boat!" she squawked excitedly. They gathered the leaves, tied them together, and hopped onto their wobbly vessel. With a few splashes and giggles, they paddled across, their laughter echoing through the forest. They had shown kindness to Brad, and now they worked together again, proving that teamwork makes adventure much more fun!

At last, they arrived at the other side, where the ground sparkled with colors more vibrant than any rainbow. As the sun began to set, a magical rainbow stretched across the sky, glowing like a giant smile. "Wow!" Brucie gasped, "It's even more beautiful than I imagined!" They each closed their eyes and made a wish together. Brucie wished for more adventures with his friends, Pippa wished for endless dance parties, and Brad, now sticky but happy, wished for more honey! The rainbow shimmered brighter, wrapping them in its colorful embrace. In that moment, they understood that the true magic lay not just in the wish itself, but in the friendship and kindness they shared along the way. And so, with giggles and dreams, the three friends returned home, ready for their next adventure!

The Festival of Colors

O nce upon a time, in a colorful little village nestled between rolling hills and sparkling streams, the Festival of Colors was about to begin. Every year, the animals of the village gathered to celebrate the arrival of spring with a grand party filled with laughter, music, and, of course, colors! This year, the wise old crab named Mr. Shellington was in charge of organizing the festival. His shell was painted with every shade imaginable, making him look like a walking rainbow. "Remember, my friends," he said, "this festival isn't just about throwing colors; it's about friendship and kindness!" The animals nodded, but some of them were already plotting to throw the most colorful splashes at each other.

As the day of the festival approached, the excitement in the air was thicker than porridge! The rabbits practiced their dancing, the birds rehearsed their songs, and even the shy little hedgehog decided to join in. However, trouble was brewing! Ming the mischievous monkey had a plan to create the biggest color explosion the village had ever seen. "Why just throw colors when you can launch them from a catapult?" he giggled, scratching his head in delight. The other animals looked concerned, but Ming just winked. "Trust me, this will be the most colorful day EVER!"

Finally, the big day arrived, and the village was bursting with energy. The sun shone brightly, and the trees seemed to sway in excitement. As the animals gathered in the central square, they donned their colorful outfits, each one more vibrant than the last. Mr. Shellington rang the bell to start the festivities. "Let the fun begin!" he declared. Suddenly, Ming, with a cheeky grin, climbed up to his catapult. He pulled the lever, and with a loud BOING, a rocket of colors shot into the air! The animals gasped, then burst into laughter as the colors rained down like a joyful rainbow. It was pure chaos, but everyone was having the time of their lives!

As the colors flew, an owl named Professor Hootsworthy took the opportunity to share a little Taoist wisdom. "You see, my friends," he hooted, "the colors represent our feelings. When we share joy and laughter, we create harmony in the world around us." The animals nodded, understanding that this festival was about more than just fun; it was a celebration of their friendship and the beauty of nature. Even Ming the monkey, who was usually full of mischief, felt a warm glow in his heart as he watched his friends play and laugh together.

As the sun began to set, painting the sky in shades of orange and pink, the animals gathered around to share stories of their favorite moments from the festival. Ming, now covered in purple and green, sheepishly admitted, "Okay, maybe the catapult was a bit much, but didn't we have fun?" Everyone agreed, and they all shared a big group hug, feeling the warmth of kindness wrap around them like a cozy blanket. That day, they learned that just like the colors of the rainbow, each one of them was unique, and together, they made the world a more beautiful place.

And so, the Festival of Colors became a cherished tradition, reminding everyone that the best adventures are those shared with friends.

The Secrets of the Bamboo Forest

The Bamboo That Could Talk

In an ancient forest, there lived a bamboo named Bambam who had a knack for talking. Ordinary? Not in Bambam's dictionary.; he was the wisest bamboo around, with a voice that could tickle your ears. He would often crack jokes that made the birds chirp with laughter and the squirrels roll on the ground, clutching their bellies. "Why did the panda bring a ladder to the bamboo grove?" he would say. "Because he wanted to reach new heights in his diet!" Bambam loved making his friends laugh, and they adored him for it.

One sunny day, a little rabbit named Brucie hopped by, looking quite glum. Bambam, noticing his long ears drooping like sad little leaves, called out, "Hey there, Brucie! Why the long face? Did you lose a carrot?" Brucie stopped, his ears perked up. "No, Bambam! It's my friend Leo the tortoise. He thinks he can never win a race against the speedy hare!" Bambam chuckled, "Well, tell Leo that slow and steady wins the race, but only if he remembers to wear his lucky socks!" With a giggle, Brucie hopped off to share Bambam's silly advice.

As the days passed, Bambam became the go-to bamboo for advice and laughter. One morning, a wise old owl named Oliver perched above Bambam and hooted, "Bambam, what do you think is the secret to happiness?" Bambam rustled his leaves and replied, "Well, Oliver, happiness is like a bamboo shoot; it grows stronger with love and kindness!" Oliver nodded, impressed by Bambam's wisdom. "You're right! But I still think I need more naps!" he hooted back. The forest echoed with laughter, and everyone agreed that a good nap was always a part of happiness.

Things took a twist when a fierce storm swept through the forest, leaving everyone a bit shaken. Bambam stood tall, comforting his friends. "Remember, my buddies, we're all like bamboo; we bend but don't break! Just hold on tight!" As the winds howled, Bambam wiggled back and forth, making it look like he was dancing. His silly moves made the frightened animals laugh, and soon, they were all swaying together. They realized that even in tough times, a little humor could lift their spirits and keep them strong.

When the storm passed, Bambam looked around at his friends, all smiling and safe. "See? We did it together! Friendship and kindness are the roots that keep us grounded, even in the wildest storms!" The animals cheered, and Brucie piped up, "Let's have a race, but this time let's see who can tell the funniest joke!" Bambam, of course, won the race with his incredible punchlines. And from that day on, the bamboo grove became a place of joy, laughter, and the best stories, all thanks to the bamboo that could talk!

The Adventures of the Silly Squirrel

O nce upon a time, in a glade of the greenest trees, there lived a silly squirrel named Sid. Not your usual nut gatherer,Sid had flair, But he also had a knack for getting into trouble. One frosty morning, he decided to explore the tallest tree in the forest, which he called the Great Oak of Wonders. With his bushy tail twitching with excitement, he scampered upward, chattering away about how he would find the biggest acorn ever. But as he climbed higher, he didn't notice that he was actually climbing straight into a nest of sleepy owls!

As Sid reached the top, he found himself face-to-face with a wide-eyed owl named Oliver, who was not amused. "Whooo are you and what are you doing in my home?" asked Oliver in his deep, sleepy voice. Sid, not one to be easily frightened, replied, "I'm just hunting for acorns, but I seem to have stumbled into a cozy owl hotel!" With a silly grin, he offered Oliver a peanut he had in his pouch, hoping to lighten the mood. To his surprise, Oliver couldn't resist the tasty treat and began to chuckle, realizing that this silly squirrel might not be so bad after all.

Their laughter attracted the attention of other forest creatures. Soon, a curious rabbit named Brucie hopped over, followed by Benny the bear, who was always on the lookout for snacks. "What's going on up here?" Brucie asked, his nose twitching with excitement. Sid, eager to impress, stood tall and exclaimed, "I'm hosting a tree-top party! Who wants to join?" Benny, with his big bear belly, laughed and said, "Count me in, as long as there are snacks!" And just like that, the Great Oak of Wonders turned into the most delightful gathering in the forest, with Sid as the silly host.

As the sun began to set, the friends shared stories, jokes, and lots of acorns. Sid realized that the best adventures aren't just

about climbing trees or finding treasures; they're about the
friends you make along the way.
With each giggle and every silly dance, Sid learned the Taoist
value of friendship, discovering
that kindness could turn even the
most unexpected encounters into
joyful memories. And so, the forest echoed with laughter, as the
silly squirrel taught everyone that
sometimes, being a little silly is
the best way to be.

From that day on, Sid became
the connector of all creatures in
the forest. He organized weekly tree-top parties where every-

one, from the tiniest ant to the biggest bear, could come together and share in the fun. They played games, exchanged stories, and learned to celebrate their differences. Through these silly adventures, Sid helped everyone understand the beauty of harmony in nature, showing that each creature, no matter how big or small, had a special role to play. And so the forest thrived, filled with laughter, friendship, and a little bit of silliness, reminding all who lived there to cherish the magic of togetherness.

The Tale of Two Turtles

The Speedy Turtle and the Slowpoke

In a sparkling forest, where the trees whispered secrets and the rivers giggled as they flowed, lived a speedy little rabbit named Brucie and a slowpoke tortoise named Tina. Brucie loved to zoom around, hopping from one flower to another, showing off his incredible speed. Tina, on the other hand, took her time, slowly munching on delicious leaves and enjoying the warm sunshine. One sunny day, Brucie challenged Tina to a race, thinking it would be the easiest win of his life. Tina just smiled and said, "Alright, but let's make it an adventure!"

As they prepared for the race, Brucie dashed around in circles, practicing his speed, while Tina calmly stretched her legs and took a deep breath. The other animals gathered to watch, excited to see who would win. "Ready, set, go!" shouted Oliver the wise old owl. Off went Brucie like a rocket, leaving Tina far behind. He zipped past trees, leaped over rocks, and giggled, thinking about how he would celebrate his victory with a big feast of carrots. Meanwhile, Tina plodded along, humming a little tune and enjoying the colorful butterflies fluttering by.

Brucie was having so much fun that he thought, "Why not take a quick nap?" He found a cozy patch of grass, plopped down, and closed his eyes. Tina, moving at her own pace, continued her journey. As she ambled along, she noticed all the beautiful things around her—the sparkling dew on the grass, the busy ants working together, and the gentle breeze that danced through the leaves. With every step, Tina felt happy and at peace, while Brucie dreamed of victory in his sleep.

After a delightful nap, Brucie awoke to the sound of cheering. "Oh no! I must be behind!" he exclaimed, racing off again. But as he got closer to the finish line, he saw Tina crossing it slowly but surely. The animals erupted in applause! Brucie couldn't believe his eyes. "How did you do that?"

he asked, panting. Tina chuckled and replied, "It's not always about speed, my friend. Sometimes, taking your time allows you to enjoy the journey."

From that day on, Brucie learned a valuable lesson about friendship and kindness. He realized that everyone has their own pace, and that's what makes the world a wonderful place. The speedy rabbit and the slowpoke tortoise became the best of friends, reminding each other to appreciate life's little moments. They spent their days exploring together, and whenever Brucie raced ahead, he would always wait for Tina to catch up, sharing stories and laughter along the way.

Lessons in Patience and Kindness

High up the mountain in a lush, green forest, lived a wise old frog named Nigel. Nigel was known for two things: his incredible patience and his love for sharing stories. One misty day, Nigel spotted a young named Rina hopping around in a frenzy, trying to gather as many carrots as she could. "Why the rush, Rina? Carrots are not going anywhere!" Nigel chuckled, watching the little bunny tumble over her own feet in her excitement.

Rina stopped and panted, her little nose twitching. "But Nigel, I need to collect all the carrots before the big feast tonight! Everyone will be there, and I want to impress my friends!" She was almost bouncing off the ground with energy. Nigel smiled, his skin shining in the sunlight. "You know, Rina, sometimes it's not about how many carrots you gather, but how much fun you have while gathering them." Rina blinked in confusion, her mind racing faster than her little legs could hop.

Determined to help her understand, Nigel slowly suggested, "Why don't we gather carrots together? I'll show you my secret way of doing things." With a curious bounce, Rina agreed. As they strolled through the garden, Nigel took his time, enjoying the vibrant colors of the flowers and the sweet sounds of the birds. "See, my friend, if you are patient, you can enjoy the beauty around you. And kindness, like sharing the experience, makes it even better." Rina giggled as she tried to keep up with Nigel's slow but steady pace.

As they collected carrots, Rina noticed how many more friends joined them, all curious about what Nigel and Rina were doing. They laughed, chatted, and shared stories as they worked together. Rina realized that with every carrot they pulled from the ground, they were also pulling together a little bit of friendship and joy. "This is way more fun than just rushing around!" she exclaimed, her little heart swelling with happiness. Nigel nodded, pleased to see Rina learning the value of patience and kindness.

When the feast finally arrived, Rina had not only gathered plenty of carrots but also made many new friends. As they all shared the delicious meal, Rina told everyone about her day with Nigel, the wise frog who taught her that sometimes, it's not the number of carrots you have that matters, but the journey and the friends you make along the way. The forest echoed with laughter, and Nigel chuckled softly, knowing he had helped plant the seeds of patience and kindness in Rina's heart, which would grow into beautiful friendships for years to come.

The Race to the Finish Line

In a vibrant forest where the trees danced with the wind, a group of animals decided to hold a race to see who could reach the ancient willow tree first. The participants included Brucie the Bunny, who was as fast as lightning, Lucy the Llama, who was as graceful as a cloud, and Gary the Gecko, who could climb anything. All the animals gathered at the starting line, their hearts pounding with excitement and their stomachs rumbling from too many pre-race snacks. Oliver the wise old owl, who was the judge, fluffed his feathers and hooted, "On your marks, get set, go!"

Brucie zipped off like a streak of fur, his little legs a blur as he hopped through the forest. Lucy trotted along, taking her time to enjoy the flowers, and Gary scurried up a tree, thinking he could glide down to the finish line. But just as Brucie was about to claim victory, he tripped over a stray acorn and tumbled into a bush. "Who put that there?" he exclaimed, shaking off leaves and feeling rather ridiculous. Meanwhile, Lucy paused to help him up, showing that kindness was more important than winning. "Let's finish this together!" she said, her eyes sparkling with determination.

As they continued the race, Gary decided to take a shortcut by leaping from branch to branch. He was feeling pretty proud until he realized he had no idea where he was! "Uh-oh," he squeaked, hanging upside down from a branch. The other animals laughed, and even Brucie, who was still a bit dizzy, couldn't help but chuckle. "Looks like you've taken a wrong turn, buddy!" he called out. Gary, hanging there like a confused fruit bat, realized he might need to ask for help to get back on track.

The race had turned into a wild adventure filled with laughter and unexpected turns. Instead of just competing, the animals discovered that working together made their journey much more enjoyable. Brucie suggested they all run together to the finish line.

"It's not about who finishes first, but about the fun we have!" he said with a grin. Lucy nodded enthusiastically, and Gary finally managed to swing down from his tree, landing right beside them. They formed a little team, hopping and trotting side by side, sharing stories and giggles as they approached the willow tree.

When they finally reached the ancient willow, they found it wrapped in colorful ribbons and surrounded by flowers. Oliver the wise old owl smiled and declared, "Congratulations! You've all won the race by showing friendship and kindness." The animals cheered and celebrated their adventure, realizing that the real treasure was the bond they had formed along the way. As they shared a picnic under the sprawling branches, they agreed that the journey was much more magical than the finish line itself, proving that in the world of Taoism, harmony and teamwork are the true victories.

The Seasons of the Little Fox

Springtime Surprises

In the heart of spring, when the flowers burst into color and the sun shines like a friendly giant, magical surprises await. One sunny morning, the wise turtle, Tao, woke up from his long winter nap, stretched his legs, and noticed something unusual. His favorite pond was bubbling with excitement! The frogs were singing their silly songs, and the fish were flipping and flopping like they were practicing for a dance competition. Tao chuckled, "What a lively bunch! I wonder what surprises spring has in store for us today!"

As Tao waddled closer to the pond, he heard a loud splash. Out popped Nigel, the mischievous little frog, wearing a tiny crown made of daisies. "Look at me, Tao! I'm King of the Pond!" Nigel croaked, leaping onto a lily pad. The other frogs cheered, but Tao raised an eyebrow. "King of the Pond? You know what that means, right? You have to be kind and share your snacks!" Nigel's eyes widened. "Snacks? I thought being king meant I could eat all the flies I wanted!" Tao smiled, "Well, that's part of it, but sharing is what makes a good king!"

Just then, a gentle breeze rustled the trees, and a fluffy cloud floated by, revealing a pair of tiny, shimmering fairies flitting about. "We're the Spring Sprites!" they chimed in unison, their laughter ringing like little bells. "We bring surprises and joy to everyone! Today, we've brought a treasure hunt!" Tao's eyes sparkled with excitement. "Oh, what a splendid idea! Let's teach Nigel about sharing and teamwork while we're at it!" The fairies sprinkled their magic dust, and suddenly, the pond was filled with colorful eggs, each hiding a special surprise.

Nigel the frog, feeling a bit nervous about being king, looked at the eggs and said, "What if I keep them all for myself?" Tao laughed, "But then you'd miss out on the fun! A true king shares his treasures with his friends." With a deep breath, Nigel nodded and called out to the other frogs. "Let's find the eggs together! Whoever finds the most gets a crown!" The frogs jumped into action, hopping and giggling, their excitement filling the air. Nigel felt a warm glow in his chest, realizing that sharing made the hunt even more magical.

As the sun began to set, Tao gathered all the frogs around him. "Today, we learned that spring brings not only surprises but also the joy of friendship and kindness. Nigel, you may be King of the Pond, but your true crown shines when you share." Nigel beamed with pride, surrounded by his friends, each wearing their own little crowns made of flowers. They all agreed that the best surprise of spring was not just the colorful eggs, but the laughter and love they shared together. And as night fell, the magical pond sparkled under the stars, filled with the promise of many more adventures to come.

Summer Shenanigans

In a small village nestled between the rolling hills of the East, summer arrived with all its warmth and splendor. The sun smiled down on the villagers, and the air buzzed with excitement. But this summer was special; it was the Summer Shenanigans Festival! Every animal in the village was invited to join in the fun, and they were all eager to show off their skills. The rabbits were preparing their famous carrot races, the birds were practicing their singing, and the wise old crab, Mr. Shellington, was planning a grand storytelling session that would leave everyone in stitches.

As the festival began, the rabbits hopped energetically around the track, their little feet thumping against the ground like a drum. But there was one rabbit, Brucie, who had a secret weapon: his super stretchy ears! Instead of racing, he decided to stretch his ears all the way to the finish line while lounging in the shade, munching on a delicious carrot. Everyone cheered and giggled as Brucie's ears crossed the finish line before he did. "I guess I'll have to work on my running skills!" he chuckled, as his friends rolled on the grass, laughing until their bellies hurt.

Meanwhile, high up in the trees, the birds were having their own hilarious competition. They were trying to sing the highest notes, but instead of sweet melodies, they sounded like a chorus of squeaky toys! Pippa, the parrot, took it upon herself to teach

everyone a song about friendship, but every time she sang, the
other birds would join in and create the silliest mix of sounds. "If
only we could sing in harmony like
the wind in the trees!" squawked,
flapping her wings in frustration.
But the laughter that filled the
air was music enough, and they
all agreed that sometimes, a little silliness is what summer is all
about.

As the sun began to set, it was
time for Mr. Shellington's storytelling hour. The animals gathered around, their eyes sparkling
with anticipation. "Tonight, I'll tell

you the tale of the Great Tortoise and the Mischievous Dragon," he announced. As he spun the story, he exaggerated every detail, making the dragon's antics even more ridiculous. "And just when the dragon thought she could scare the tortoise, she tripped over her own tail and landed in a pond!" The audience erupted in laughter, and even the shyest animals couldn't hold back their giggles. Mr. Shellington reminded everyone that even the mightiest can stumble, and it's okay to laugh at ourselves.

As the festival came to a close, the animals realized that the best part of Summer Shenanigans wasn't winning or being the best; it was the friendships they built and the laughter they shared. They learned that in Taoism, just as in nature, balance is key. The silly moments and the fun adventures helped them grow closer together. As they settled down under the twinkling stars, they made a promise to carry the joy of summer with them all year long, embracing every season with the same spirit of friendship and kindness. And from that day forward, they knew that every summer would be filled with shenanigans, laughter, and a little bit of magic.

Autumn Adventures and Winter Wonders

As the leaves began to turn shades of orange, red, and gold, the magical forest came alive with excitement. Sid the squirrel and Benny the bear were planning their autumn adventure. "Let's race to the top of the tallest tree!" Sid squeaked, his fluffy tail twitching with anticipation. Benny, who was more interested in a cozy nap than a race, replied with a chuckle, "Only if you promise not to nibble on my paws if I win!" The two friends laughed, for they knew that whether Sid climbed the tree first or Benny took a leisurely stroll, their friendship would always be the best prize of all.

As they dashed through the rustling leaves, they noticed a peculiar sight. A group of tiny, giggling fairies were playing hide-and-seek among the pumpkins. "I bet they think they're the best hiders in the whole forest!" Benny said, his belly shaking with laughter. Sid decided to join the fairies, leaping from branch to branch, while Benny plopped down next to a pumpkin. "I'll be the judge! Whoever gets caught has to share their candy!" he called out. It turned into a hilarious game where everyone forgot about winning and focused on having fun, proving that kindness and laughter are the true treasures of autumn.

As the days grew shorter and the chill of winter crept in, the forest transformed into a sparkling wonderland. Benny and Sid bundled up in scarves made from colorful leaves. "Do you think the snow will be as deep as my belly?" Benny pondered aloud, his eyes twinkling with mischief. Sid chattered excitedly, "Let's find out! We can build the biggest snowman the forest has ever seen!" With that, they rolled snowballs, stacking them high, until their creation resembled a wobbly giant with a carrot nose and a floppy hat made of pine needles.

But then, a gust of wind sent their snowman tumbling down!

"Oh no! Our snowman!" cried Sid. Benny burst into laughter and said, "Maybe he just wanted to do a snow dance!" So, they joined in, twirling and spinning in the soft snow, creating a flurry of laughter and joy. It didn't matter that their snowman was gone; what mattered was the happiness they shared and the memories they made together. That's the magic of winter—turning mishaps into adventures!

As the seasons changed, Sid and Benny learned important lessons about balance and harmony in nature. They realized that just like the forest, their friendship needed a little bit of both—sometimes being silly like a squirrel, and sometimes cozy like a bear. They understood that each season brought its own adventures and wonders, teaching them about kindness, laughter, and the joy of sharing. With every autumn wind and winter snowflake, they celebrated their unique friendship, knowing that together, they could explore the magical world around them.

The Balance of Yin and Yang

The Day and Night Dance

Once upon a time in a magical forest, there lived a wise old turtle named Tofu and a playful little rabbit named Brucie. Tofu had a shell that sparkled like the stars, and Brucie had ears so long they could almost touch the clouds. These two friends loved to dance, but there was one little problem: Tofu liked to dance during the day, while Brucie only felt like dancing at night. It was the start of what the animals called "The Day and Night Dance," a dance that would go down in history as the funniest dance-off ever!

One sun drenched morning, Tofu decided to throw a big dance party. He invited everyone in the forest, including the twirling squirrels, the hopping frogs, and the clapping birds. Brucie, however, was still snoozing under a shady tree, dreaming of moonlit adventures. When Tofu started to shake his shell and wiggle his little webbed turtle feet , all the animals cheered! But Brucie missed the whole thing! When he finally woke up and saw the party was over, he jumped around, asking, "Where is everyone? Did I miss the fun?"

Feeling a little sad, Brucie decided to have his own dance party at night. He invited all his friends, including Tofu, who was still napping. As the moon rose high, Brucie danced and twirled under the glowing stars. His long ears flopped around like two silly ribbons. The owls hooted along, and even the sleepy raccoons couldn't resist joining the fun. But when Tofu finally woke up from his nap, he found himself alone in the dark. "Where is everyone? Did I miss the fun again?" he wondered, scratching his head with his tiny webbed feet.

Finally, one day, Tofu and Brucie met up to share their dance stories. Brucie laughed, "You danced in the sun while I was busy dreaming!" Tofu chuckled back, "And you danced under the moon while I was counting stars!" They both realized that they had been missing out on each other's fun. So, they came up with a brilliant idea. "What if we had a dance party that started at sunset and ended at sunrise?" they exclaimed together.

From that day on, the Day and Night Dance became the most magical event in the forest. Animals from near and far would gather as Tofu kicked off the party with his slow and steady turtle moves, while Brucie followed with his wild and wiggly rabbit hops. They took turns, making sure everyone could join in, and the forest was filled with laughter, joy, and a little bit of silliness. And so, the balance of day and night, just like the balance of yin and yang, created a beautiful harmony that brought all the animals closer together, proving that friendship can shine brightly no matter the time of day!

The Tale of the Happy Sun and the Sleepy Moon

In a land where the sky sparkled like a treasure chest full of diamonds, there lived a cheerful sun named Sunny and a drowsy moon named Moony. Sunny was always giggling and shining brightly, making flowers bloom and birds sing.

"Look at me!" he would shout, spreading his rays like a big, warm hug. Meanwhile, Moony was like a sleepy kitten, always yawning and drifting between dreams of floating on fluffy clouds. "Oh, dear," she would mumble, "is it night already? I think I need just five more minutes!"

Sunny loved to wake up early, racing across the sky to greet the day. He would play hide-and-seek with the clouds, painting the sky in shades of orange and pink. "Catch me if you can!" he would tease the fluffy clouds, who would puff and giggle in response. But when it was time for Moony to rise, she would stretch and say, "Five more minutes, please!" And while Sunny would dance around, Moony would stumble out of her moon bed, her hair still tangled from sleep.

"Why do you always have to be so bright and cheery, Sunny?" she asked, rubbing her eyes.

One day, Sunny decided it was time to shake things up a bit. "Let's swap places!" he exclaimed with a twinkle in his eye. Moony blinked in surprise, her sleepy face brightening up a little. "But I've never been a sun before!"

she replied, her voice a mix of excitement and hesitation. "And I've never been a moon!" Sunny laughed. "It'll be an adventure! Plus, we can see how the other half lives!" So, with a magical twist of fate, the Happy Sun and the Sleepy Moon switched roles for one day.

As Sunny floated through the night sky, he tried to be a good moon. He glowed softly, but every time he laughed, he accidentally turned the night into day! The stars were flabbergasted, saying, "Hey, Sunny, we like our night-time disco parties!" Meanwhile, Moony, trying her best to shine bright as the sun, found herself dozing off while painting sunrises. "Oops! Sorry, flowers!" she mumbled, as the daisies were left half-sprouted and the tulips yawned wide open.

At the end of their adventurous day, Sunny and Moony met back in the sky, both giggling and blushing. "I think I prefer being the sun!" Sunny chuckled, while Moony nodded in agreement, "And I think I'm better at being the moon, especially with my cozy dreams." They realized that while they may be different, their friendship brought out the best in each other. And from that day on, Sunny and Moony danced through the sky, learning to appreciate their unique gifts and the harmony they created together, reminding everyone that it's our differences that make the world a wonderful place.

Finding Balance in Fun and Rest

Finding balance in fun and rest is like trying to juggle a bunch of squirmy frogs while riding a unicycle! Just when you think you've got it all figured out, one of those frogs hops away, and suddenly you're in a wobbly mess. In the magical world of Taoism, the wise old turtles always say that too much fun can wear you out, while too much resting can make you feel like a sleepy sloth. So, how can we find that perfect balance? Well, let's dive into some more enchanting tales!

Once upon a time in a lush bamboo forest, there lived a lively little monkey named Ming. Ming loved to swing and play, jumping from tree to tree with the grace of a flying squirrel. But there was one tiny problem: Ming never wanted to take a break! His friends, the wise old owl and the gentle deer, tried to convince him to rest. "Ming," hooted the owl, "you can't just play all day! You need to recharge your batteries!" But Ming just laughed, "Batteries? I'm a monkey! I run on bananas!"

One sunny afternoon, after a day filled with endless swinging and jumping, Ming found himself feeling groggy. He tried to play tag with the other animals, but instead of zooming around, he stumbled and fell into a pile of leaves. "Oooof!" he exclaimed, shaking the leaves off his head. "Maybe a little rest wouldn't hurt." With the wise owl's advice ringing in his ears, Ming decided to take a nap, and soon he was dreaming of banana trees dancing in the breeze!

Meanwhile, in the same forest, there was a tortoise named Tina who adored taking long, leisurely naps. Tina was the queen of relaxation, but she often missed out on all the fun. One day, while Tina snoozed under a shady tree, her friends played games nearby. When she finally woke up, the sun was setting, and the laughter of her friends felt like a distant echo. Tina realized that while resting is important, so is joining in on the fun! "I guess I can stretch my legs a little!" she chuckled to herself.

Ming and Tina soon learned that balancing fun and rest is like making a delicious soup. You need just the right amount of ingredients! They decided to create a daily schedule: a little time for swinging and a little time for snoozing. They even invented a game called "Sleepy Swing," where they took turns swinging for a while and then resting under the trees, sharing stories and laughter. The other animals joined in, and soon the entire forest was filled with giggles and sleepy yawns.

In the end, Ming and Tina became the great friends, proving that finding balance is all about enjoying both playtime and nap time. They learned that life is more magical when you take time to have fun and also time to rest. And so, in the heart of the bamboo forest, the animals discovered that the secret to happiness lies in the dance between adventure and relaxation, just like the gentle ebb and flow of nature itself!

The End... Or Is It Just the Beginning?

Well, here we are, friend. The end of Magical Beasts of the East. You've danced with dragons, giggled with monkeys, and probably wondered at least once, "Why is that turtle taking so long to finish his sentence?" (Spoiler: turtles always take their time.)

But let's be real for a second—did you think this was just a book of stories? Oh no, my clever little reader! This was actually a super-secret adventure training manual disguised as a storybook. That's right! You've been learning ancient Taoist wisdom without even realizing it. Boom! Mind blown, right?

So, what have we discovered together? Dragons can dance (and occasionally set things on fire while twirling). Monkeys might not always have the best plans, but they sure know how to make life interesting. Tortoises are wise, slow, and... let's face it... probably better at life than all of us. And bamboo? Turns out, it's not just panda snacks—it's basically nature's stand-up comedian.

But here's the sneaky, magical part: these weren't just stories about magical creatures. They were little lessons about kindness, balance, and going with the flow—like leaves floating down a river or ice cream melting down your hand on a hot day (hey, it happens to the best of us).

And now comes the most important part: YOU! Yes, you with the peanut butter smudge on your cheek and the crumpled blanket over your shoulders. What will you do with these lessons? Will you share your last cookie with your little sibling? Will you slow down and enjoy a sunset like Tina the tortoise? Or maybe, just maybe, you'll start your very own dragon dance party in the living room (permission from grown-ups recommended unless you want to explain a broken lamp).

But before we say goodbye, let me let you in on one final secret: this isn't really "The End." Nope, not even close. Because every time you're kind to a friend, every time you laugh so hard your juice comes out of your nose, and every time you take a moment to just be—you're living your own magical story.

So go out there, little adventurer. Chase sunsets, share your snacks, and, most importantly, remember: sometimes the biggest magic isn't in spells or treasures—it's in the little moments you share with others.

And if you ever miss your dragon buddies or wise old turtles, don't worry—you can always flip back to page one and start the adventure all over again.

Now, close this book, give yourself a little pat on the back (seriously, you've earned it), and go make the world a little brighter... one giggle, one dance move, and one dragon-sized smile at a time.

The End (but also, The Beginning).

Let's Meet
Psalm

Psalm Carnoustie is a passionate children's author dedicated to introducing young readers to the vibrant world of cultures, religions, and timeless wisdom from around the globe. With a warm and engaging storytelling style, Psalm crafts tales that spark curiosity, foster understanding, and celebrate diversity.

Believing that children are the seeds of a more compassion-ate future, Psalm is driven by the philosophy that early expo-sure to different beliefs and tra-ditions nurtures empathy, kind-ness, and open-mindedness. Her books serve as gentle guides, helping children see the beauty in differences while embracing the common threads that unite us all.

When she's not weaving enchant-ing stories, Psalm enjoys explor-ing cultural festivals, collecting folklore from faraway lands, and sharing moments of quiet reflec-tion in nature. Her stories are not just books—they are bridges, connecting little hearts to a world of understanding and acceptance.